There We Go

Elizabeth Chapman

Cataloguing-in-Publications entry is available from the National Library of Australia http:/catalogue.nla.gov.au

First edition published 2021

For our beloved son Hugo,

there aren't enough words to describe our love for you.

Also, in loving memory of Hugo's little friend,

Micah James.

He smiles at empty spaces,

coos at the ceiling,

the cornice, the wall...

He settles, staring at empty spaces,

for he sees something

where I see nothing at all.

If I could hold you all night, I would.

Tiny hands wrapped around fingers.

But I need my sleep and you need yours.

So till tomorrow, my little love,

when we do it all again.

My greatest fears

wrapped in one so small.

This heart can't bare them alone,

so I surrender all.

Our battle begins

through the bottle,

through the moments before sleep.

Then a sigh.

Nestled in,

off you drift.

I miss you.

Already.

So I gaze at photographs

till you wake.

Forgive me –

sometimes Mummy

gets lost in routine.

Then I see you

smile brightly

and I know

you are where

I'm meant to be.

Tugboats, duckies, and sea creatures...

As you dream,

your daddy pours me a glass of wine

to unwind in the bubbles.

I smile. For all I see?

Tugboats, duckies, and sea creatures.

If this flawed heart

explodes with makeshift

mortal affection

then never could I fathom

His eternal love

for you, little one.

Teddy bear socks on the nightstand.

Bibs – everywhere –

(except when we need one)

Rainbow toys on the beige couch.

Order – nowhere –

I love being his mum.

Late night...

Routine?

Shot.

Life happened...

Moments

Not to be forgot.

I let my coffee go cold for you.

Not because I want to.

But because my want to hold you

is so much greater.

I kiss you in your sleep.

You smile –

still dreaming.

And in that moment,

it's everything.

My heart aches for you.

Even while you sleep,

I feel the pull.

My heart prays for you.

Even through the restless nights,

my heart is full.

I lay here

listening to you breathe

and wonder,

what you will be?

For you,

my little one,

are extraordinary.

You're here

in this broken world

and I now know what it's like

to "pray ceaselessly"

Oh little one,

how loved you are,

your angels gather in the sky.

Oh Holy One,

Creator of stars,

watch over your lamb this night.

Your sweet face grounds me.

Skin to skin, it soothes me.

Hold my hand a little longer,

my little love.

I may be your safe place

but you are also mine.

Strawberry fingers

– sticky and sweet –

stained summer pink

just like your cheeks.

Let us lay here a moment longer,

some place between smiles and dreams.

Let me gaze, dear, a moment longer,

sweet face between smiles and dreams.

Orange sweeps a glowing sky

– another sunrise drive.

While most of the world sleeps,

so do you... in the car seat.

I wrap you in prayer before you sleep

from your downy hair to your squidgy feet.

I wrap you in prayer from your blessed birth,

grateful for all your days on this earth.

I wrap you in prayer that you may know

the Lord's peace as you rest and grow.

I wrap you in prayer for all that will be,

for all the adventures I cannot see.

We disappear, you and I

– it's our favourite party trick.

When the noisy world comes rolling by,

we escape to where it's quiet.

And there we stay with squishy cuddles

dribbly kisses and snuggles.

Pillow splattered with milky puddles

beneath the invisible blanket.

In the year that was, God gave us you,

and now we're three instead of two.

In the year that was, the world grew still,

while our world thrived in wonderous thrills.

In the year that was, so bittersweet,

you laughed and waved and grew four teeth.

In the year that was, you captured hearts

with joy-filled eyes so bright and smart.

So the year that was could not be bad.

It may just be the best we've had.

Mummy is craving winter rain,

she's waiting for our quiet days.

Where you and I have nowhere to go

but play and nap and dream of snow.

We'll watch the world go about its troubles

while curled up in our little bubble.

Beneath the old chair,

by the light of a polar bear,

a boy no bigger than his book

made for himself a reading nook.

On Sunday afternoon,

when no one was there,

we sprawled on the floor

with books and bears.

Off on adventures

with Gigi and Karl

– that giraffe and sage dog

made us stay a good while!

Nectarine kisses by the big old tree.

A half for you and a half for me.

Picked and eaten, fresh and sweet,

sunrise fruit, we eat and eat.

Till Summer's sun sends us in,

our cheeks rosy with nectarine.

Peek-a-boo, Sunlight!

Dim grey. Bright white.

Fluttering curtain –

Fist scrunched so tight.

Where are you, Sunlight?

No nap. Play time!

Peak-a-boo, Sunlight!

Before it's night.

Slow down, Sweetheart

Standing so tall

Slow down, Sweetheart

Sponging it all

Slow down, Sweetheart

With firsts and lasts

Slow down, Sweetheart

Don't grow too fast

Oh to see the world through your child eyes

Enchantment. Wonder. Angels in the sky.

Our little house, your castle. Your kingdom, the backyard.

No game left unplayed. No quest deemed too hard.

We lay our battles outside the door.

Like yesterday. And the night before.

We're a little bruised – you and I.

Our weariness shows in low light.

But lullabies sing our hearts awake,

cheek to chest, new mercies await.

All is forgotten from the day that was

and all that matters is now, because

even with angels standing by,

I hesitate to say goodnight.

How I wish she'd known you,

my fair-haired blue-eyed boy.

She'd coddle you and kiss you

if this was another time.

But just as she was gone,

your little life appeared.

And just as I was grieving,

God's love shone so clear.

And now I see in you

the joy of whom I loved.

I pray one day you meet

beyond the clouds above.

Under the weather. Just not yourself.

It wouldn't be obvious to everyone else.

But your smile is weaker, your bright eyes grey.

Life just won't play its usual game.

Something's not right in your little world,

so we'll snuggle and sleep until you return.

On our knees before the throne,

by the One who has atoned,

through the Holy Spirit within,

Heavenly Father, please save him.

How can I know you forever,

when yesterday you arrived?

This beautiful season of us

has changed the essence of time.

And to think it was you all along

every kick, every joy, every fear.

We had waited for a miracle

and you're our answered prayer.

So on this day we remember

the year that has gone by,

unbelieving in every way

this precious gift of time.

You see me dishevelled and tired

on those five-coffee days.

You see me in trackpants and slippers

and you always smile anyway.

But then there are those moments

when Mummy dresses up

and you pay special attention.

Your sparkling eyes light up!

And in those flickering moments,

my heart may skip a beat.

For, like me, you notice

life's lovely little things.

We're both tired, but you hide it better.

You play while Mummy lays her head on a bear.

On the rug. On the floor.

You play till you can't play anymore.

Then you pull up a bear.

Well, I do. But you lay on it.

The light is dim, perfect for bedtime stories.

But there we are, Mumma and Bubba,

snuggling on bears till we're almost asleep.

Then we try our routine again.

You overflow my arms now

and eat three meals a day.

You pitter patter down the hall

and mumble as you play.

You will change, come morning,

so let's enjoy today.

While you're still the littlest

you'll ever be again.

Barefoot in my party dress,

putting you to sleep.

All dressed up, somewhere to go,

but you just want me.

Your fingers snag my styled hair

and touch my lipsticked mouth.

And there we stay, till heavy eyes

sign Mumma's one night out.

Your friend went to heaven before you could play.

Before your friend even knew his own name,

it was written in the Lamb's Book of Life.

When your friend went to heaven, you saw us cry

and pray on the phone with his daddy that night.

None of us can fathom the reason why –

your friend went to heaven.

Autumn babe blooming in rain or sun.

Why should he walk, when he can run?

Mama worries, watching him fly.

She prays to Jesus, so angels stand by.

"Please watch over our Autumn babe."

Then Mama prays the same again.

One day I'll gaze back and miss these days,

watching you learn every time you play.

When you caught my eye and took my finger,

led me to your world where I could linger...

learning your ways, soaking you in,

the sunlight catching your baby soft skin.

One day I'll gaze back and won't remember

the sleep I never had. But your world... forever.

There we go, there we go. There we go, little Hugo

There we go, there we go. There we go, my little love

There we go, there we go. Mummy loves you, dear Hugo

There we go, there we go. Angels watch from up above.

There we go, off to sleep

Till the sun says "good morning"

There we go, now let's dream

Till the moon says "good night"

There we go, there we go. Daddy loves you, dear Hugo.

There we go, there we go. Jesus wrap you in His love.

There we go, there we go. God be with you, dear Hugo.

There we go, there we go. Holy Spirit guide your heart.

There we go, off to sleep

Till the birds sing "good morning"

There we go, now let's dream

Till the stars sing "good night"

to the tune of "Brahms' Lullaby"

'...my heart is always full and overflowing with thanks to God for you as I constantly remember you in my prayers. I pray that the Father of glory, the God of our Lord Jesus Christ, would impart to you the riches of the Spirit of wisdom and the Spirit of revelation to know him through your deepening intimacy with him. I pray that the light of God will illuminate the eyes of your imagination, flooding you with light, until you experience the full revelation of the hope of his calling—that is, the wealth of God's glorious inheritances that he finds in us, his holy ones! I pray that you will continually experience the immeasurable greatness of God's power made available to you through faith. Then your lives will be an advertisement of this immense power as it works through you! This is the mighty power that was released when God raised Christ from the dead and exalted him to the place of highest honour and supreme authority in the heavenly realm! And now he is exalted as first above every ruler, authority, government, and realm of power in existence! He is gloriously enthroned over every name that is ever praised, not only in this age, but in the age that is coming!'

Ephesians 1:16-21

www.ingramcontent.com/pod-product-compliance
Lightning Source LLC
Chambersburg PA
CBHW030640150426
42811CB00072B/1933